READ-DOOR

COV·Ag→ NOSE

OTHER BOOKS BY OUR EDITORS

By Johanna Shapiro
TEXTBOOK:
The Inner World of Medical Students:
Listening to Their Voices in Poetry (2009)

By Frank L. Meyskens, Jr.
POETRY:
Aching for Tomorrow (2007)
Believing in Today (2014)

By Thelma T. Reyna
FICTION:
The Heavens Weep for Us and Other Stories (2009)

POETRY:
Breath & Bone (2011)
Hearts in Common (2013)
Rising, Falling, All of Us (2014)
Reading Tea Leaves After Trump (2018)
Dearest Papa: A Memoir in Poems (2020)

AS EDITOR:
Altadena Poetry Review: Anthology 2015
Altadena Poetry Review: Anthology 2016
When the Virus Came Calling: COVID-19 Strikes America (2020)

Doctor Poets & Other Healers

COVID in Their Own Words

Poems & Personal Essays Edited by

Thelma T. Reyna
Frank L. Meyskens, Jr.
Johanna Shapiro

Published by Golden Foothills Press
Pasadena, CA 91104
www.GoldenFoothillsPress.com
GoldenFoothillsPress@yahoo.com

ISBN 978-1-7372481-0-1

Cover photo: "Close-angel-wear-medical-masks-coronavirus." Item ID: 1840255744. From www.shutterstock.com
AUTHORS' GALLERY photos and photos in ABOUT THE EDITORS: provided by the authors and editors directly to publisher in color format. Reformatted and converted to black & white by Kevin Poythress.
Book design: Thelma T. Reyna
Cover design: Thelma T. Reyna & Kevin Poythress

Printed in the United States of America

First Edition: 2022

Advance Praise

"Tears came to my eyes as I read the first poem. Here, in this vital anthology, we hear the voices of those who have done the most to try to heal us and see us through this pandemic. The essays take the phrases from the news and political and scientific debates and lay them brick by brick across the page as we learn how the health care workers survived and learned to walk the halls of hospitals with some vestige of hope again. But it is the poems that really witness to the feelings we could not feel at the time--because it was too raw, too real, too sad, too senseless. A collective trauma: in essence, that is what this volume bears witness to and gives us a vision of healing."

--Cassie Premo Steele, PhD
National Award-Winning Poet
Author of *We Heal from Memory*

"For anyone seeking to find meaning beyond the pain, fear, and solitude experienced by healthcare providers, this book reveals the hope, commitment, and solutions for survival that lie beneath. By exposing the souls of our cherished healthcare providers, human touch and caring save the day. A must-read for anyone who is in a caring profession."

-- Adey M. Nyamathi, ANP, PhD, FAAN
Founding Dean and Distinguished Professor
Sue & Bill Gross School of Nursing
University of California, Irvine

"Reading this book at one sitting was a bit cathartic. I found the poems, and especially the essays, to be really powerful. Johanna Shapiro's anecdotal story of daily praying on a high cul-de-sac hill will be stuck in my mind . The collection builds to an unexpected crescendo…with one piece seeming to reinforce and inform another, producing a cohesive and mystical experience through reading, sharing, and remembering."

--Carolyn Clark, PhD
Writing Teacher & Poet Leader
Author of *Poet Duet: A Mother and Daughter*

"In this moving anthology of poems and short prose pieces, witnesses to the pandemic and to other crises in care document the efforts of healing, the pain of loss, the struggles of chronic illness, and the power of hugging. Death and beauty share a table furnished with IKEA chairs, whose assembly provides insight into what we learn, and don't learn, from experience."

--Julia Reinhard Lupton, PhD
Professor of English
University of California, Irvine
Author of *Shakespeare Dwelling: Designs for the Theater of Life*

"This book is a courageous, beautiful collection of writings that reveal powerful physical and psychological therapeutic transformations in both patient and healer."

--Alejandro Morales, PhD
Professor Emeritus
University of California, Irvine
Author of *Zapote Tree* , a poetry collection

"This anthology offers an opportunity to read in real time what these generous, exhausted, dedicated *Doctor Poets & Other Healers* have to say. Myriad voices populate this rich time capsule of those who strive to meet the pressing medical needs during the pandemic, sometimes at the expense of their and their families' own health and safety. The poems and essays contained are urgent, moving, and vary from right in the belly of the medical crisis, to a rare moment of reflection away from their practice. An essential, vibrant, at times painful, artifact that will leave a lasting impact."

--Carla R. Sameth
Award-Winning Writer
Author of *One Day on the Gold Line*

Doctor Poets & Other Healers

COVID in Their Own Words

To the healthcare workers of America.
You are our heroes.

Preface:
From the Editors

By Johanna Shapiro, PhD

Physicians have always written, and some of them have written poetry (Chekhov, Keats, William Carlos Williams, and Mikhail Bulgakov come to mind). In the 20th and 21st centuries, physician writing has proliferated, with many physicians recognized as popular writers and many medical journals publishing personal narratives and poetry.

If, as narratologists assert, we are basically story-telling creatures, then we all exist, at least in part, to tell our own and others' stories. As Tony Milsanek[1] has said so well, "Physicians live inside other people's stories." And because these people are their patients, these are often stories of suffering.

In our more romantic moments, some of us may once have fantasized that words on paper might be beautiful enough or meaningful enough to somehow compensate for the horrors of suffering. I suspect that life has long since disabused us of that notion. Writing does not change suffering.

Yet physicians, nurses, and other healthcare professionals continue to write. Why? Sometimes writing about a difficult event is an act of healing or atonement. It is a way of facing a painful moment (perhaps a failure of judgment or an actual medical error), coming to terms with it, and finding a place for it so that one can, if not move on, move forward. Writing can also be an act of witnessing, testifying to the painful reality of an event. "This happened; do not forget." For some, writing memorializes an especially cherished or annoying patient. Sometimes physician writers hope that writing will lead to action that will change oppressive systems, make things better, more just, less wrong. Sometimes physicians do indeed hope to create something beautiful or meaningful, to "balance out," so to speak, the grim realities of their lives.

And sometimes doctors, like the rest of us, put words on paper because that is all they, and we, have.

----

[1] Tony Miksanek, MD. *"Seven Reasons Why Doctors Write."* In *LIT MED MAGAZINE* (http://www.nyu.edu).

By Frank L. Meyskens, Jr., MD

The field of health and illness began as an ancient art based on movement and non-movement caused by injury or illness. Physicians as the primary caregiver began over two thousand years ago with the Hippocratic Oath, which itself can be interpreted as a poetic expression of the responsibilities of caregiving.

Medicine evolved from observational opinion to observations enhanced by anatomic understanding of movement, and then of the underlying principles of biological understanding of health and illness. And as this understanding progressed, both scientists and physicians found that narration alone was inadequate to explore deeper understandings of both nature and man.

And hence the emergence of the existential dialogue communicated through poetic expression. Over time, a broad range of healthcare providers emerged. With this increased diversity in specialties came diversity in expression and openness to exploring different forms of writing to communicate medical professionals' emotions, opinions, and concerns they experienced in their practice.

In 2018, my co-editor, Dr. Johanna Shapiro, and I organized the first Annual Symposium on Healing and Hope with strong sponsorship from the Chancellor's Illuminations Initiative at University of California, Irvine, where Dr. Shapiro and I both taught in the medical school. The event was well-received, and we continued it annually until 2021. That year, we emphasized diversity and inclusion and were fortunate to have poet Thelma Reyna join our event as the Keynote Speaker.

This concurrence of events led Dr. Shapiro and me to invite Dr. Reyna to serve with us as a Co-Coordinator of the 5th annual Hope and Healing Symposium, scheduled for February 2022, with themes of the ongoing impact of COVID, grief, loss, and resilience. The event features poetry and personal essays written by medical practitioners in a wide variety of fields, such as physicians, nurses, psychotherapists, home healthcare workers, medical students, and interns. This book, *Doctor Poets & Other Healers*, was birthed as part of this effort to document and understand the pandemic as our heroic healers have experienced it.

By Thelma T. Reyna, PhD

"Thank God for our poets, here in the mildness of April and in the winter storms alike, who help us find the words our own tongues feel too swollen to speak," wrote Margaret Renkl in an essay for the *New York Times* this past spring. Indeed, for poets have been in the front lines of momentous human events since the infant days of civilization.

When the coronavirus pandemic struck America in early 2020, the tsunami of illness not only sent us into sequestration, it loosed our elemental fears of suffering and death, as we lost over half-a-million souls to COVID in less than a year. Poets documented daily life and loss, gave voice to grief spreading indiscriminately, captured the monumental upending of our "normal" lives. Other writers, too, of course, alongside the classic frontliners saving lives each day, keeping our nation on its feet, providing food. "Frontliner" is now a synonym for "hero."

Perhaps the most traumatized of our fellow human beings navigating these straits of suffering were those tasked with healing: paramedics, nurses, physicians, nursing home caregivers, grief counselors . . . professionals who saw sickness and death up close and tried to stop, or mitigate, it every day. They had, not front-row seats, but *bedsides* as their vantage point; they had hand-holding, empathy, and selflessness, often stretched to a breaking point.

This anthology shows us what these healers witnessed, how they reacted, what they did to comfort those suffering, and—most meaningfully—how their own humanity was impacted by their work. How did they find solace? How were they able to go on, day after day? In this book, we hear directly from healthcare professionals, mostly in poetry they wrote in their free time, and sometimes in heartfelt personal essays written after long days of work.

Let us listen to their voices. Let us hear their broken hearts and see their tears. Their written works here, assembled as the pandemic concluded its second year of devastation in America, are essential to our collective understanding of our COVID tragedy and to the monumental recovery that lies ahead.

Table of Contents

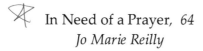
17

SCARY
SAD

Anatomy Reflections
by Riya Bansal

Forgive me, dear sir
Forgive me for
> Not being able to look into your eyes
> And knowing their color
> As I use mine to observe your hues

Forgive me for
> Not knowing your name
> Or to whom your heart belongs
> Before it was ours

Forgive me for
> Pushing the scalpel deeper
> Into skin that you spent years thickening
> Pulling all my weight against your ribs
> Cracking open that which kept you protected

Forgive me for
> Crinkling my face
> As the sharp smell fills my nose
> A small sacrifice for us
> A large sacrifice from you

Forgive me for
> Leaving to go home
> And wash off the day
> And continue on
> Without even knowing your name

A Poem for Matthew

by Erica Duh

Our shared love language felt severed too soon,

Hugs left by the wayside as the unknown loomed.

But you kept my soul cared for,

Left me food at my door,

Little messages by phone,

Keeping our child fed, cared for, so that I could rest alone.

I want to return the favor and speak in tongues you love,

Write you poems,

Words to peel away s l o w l y,

As the rest of the world surges.

When I cannot be there at your side in the coming…

Days

Weeks

Months…

I am trying to revel in new ways to show you, though we are apart,

that you are loved.

In Praise of Home School

by Anna Dunlap

I see my neighbor through the mulberry tree.
Usually in suit & heels at a desk downtown,
now she's home in baggy sweats, intent
on deconstructing a pile of delivery boxes
creating a cardboard idol to order.

On a walk, a grey brush rabbit
sits half-in, half-out of a hedge.
His nose pulsates; mine feels
red & hot under a makeshift mask.
I give him social distance, as he
waits for what might happen next.

This stretch of isolation conjures
images from childhood, when time
was a pleasure to kill – swaying
in a hammock of faded quilts, absorbed
in the lackadaisical dance of clouds,
casements of mind open wide.

Some say shelter-at-home is a wasteland
of boredom bathed in cathode rays
of ruminating on things long hid —
slackened bonds of coupledom,
slender reeds of habit,
how family depletes us.

I say—we are being home-schooled.
The world has been too fast,
too loud, too much for too long.
We are blinking, peering at the
frightened eyes of the front-line,
the carnage of the microscopic,
the myth of endless progress.

Praise the lesson: earth is not ours.
We are not master of anything.

A Letter to My Future Self

by Michael Eselun

Dear Michael,

Oh, how I long for answers from you! Do we make it? You and I? What losses have you endured? I want to steal the teacher's copy of the textbook from behind her desk to see the answers in the back.

But what do I even mean when I ask, "Did we make it?" As if there is a finish line? A point when it's over—this chapter? When it all goes back to the way it was before? As if this is as finite, as discrete as the last agonizing semester of eighth grade? I suppose I see it that way from here, though I know it's not. In a way, just as I never quite "got over" the trauma of eighth grade, perhaps this trauma, too, will never leave me.

Maybe it shouldn't. I hope it doesn't. May I be shaped by it. But just tell me—*Will it be OK?*

Of course it will. It is now. I know that, too. And I want you to know when you remember me, when you conjure up these times in your memory, that a part of me knew that, too.

Michael

Ikea U
by Michael Eselun

I bought those two simple white kitchen chairs from Ikea for my mom. Such a straightforward design—how hard could it be to assemble them?

I laid out all the wood segments and pieces. I emptied the bags of washers, bolts, and specialty spacers and began to study the directions. Assembling and tightening the first few joints seemed to take hours. So much cursing. By the time I came to the last joint on the last chair, I was an expert. Now! Now, I know how to do this! Just in time to never need this skill again.

There are those eternally optimistic—"spiritual"– folks, who have likened this pandemic to a golden opportunity to hit the reset button for life on earth, to slow down and sift the absolutely essential from all the extraneous. A spiritual rebirth for the planet. A complete shift of perspective.

Not me.

I guess a part of me would like to think so. That this time, if we survive it, will be a distillation… a refinement of the wisdom and the skill of survival, handed down across the generations and gleaned through our experience. My experience. My own parents lived through the Great Depression and World War II, after all. When they were in the middle of it, no one knew that these calamities would ever end. We knew they ended from the first moment we were taught about those times. It was history. I would like to believe that what I learn along the way will only come in handy for the next challenge—be essential in fact. A kind of faith in that concept has seen me through life so far. A faith in growth. If only a faith that that growth would be its own reward. What if I don't believe in that anymore?

What if it's like assembling kitchen chairs from Ikea? Once you assemble the chair and have a seat—having faced the frustration, and endured— the skill is now lost. Useless? We just throw away the box it came in.

And we sit.

And we wait.

Isolation

by Chloie Limpin Flores

1.

The brilliant light of a newborn day
crawled into the convalescent room
where the mother, despite her pain, stood up to say
"Please open the windows wide."

With latex hands, I revealed the outside
where soft cotton sailed through the blue.
To my delight, she waved to a child passing by
whose father waved back too.

She's watching the world from behind a glass,
quarantined by a merciless sickness.
Sometimes the best I can do is listen,
to comfort, to soothe, to understand.

I spend the hours performing little tasks
that ease my patients' loneliness.
I swaddle their worry, nurse them with care,
become their loving confidante.

While I cannot heal disease, I help them feel
they matter in this world.
I can't be their baby, their daughter,
their sister or wedded partner,
but I feed them, bathe them, and honor them
in the time we share, each day, each shift.

2.

When the hours matured to somber twilight,
I wended my way back home.
My service wasn't finished yet:
I took care of my sick grandmother.

It was hard to see her suffer,
and hear our conversations run short,
but every battle made her tougher,
and she'd humbly praise my support.

Her daughters and sons were unable to come,
from lands beyond the deserts and seas.
How ignorant the world has become
with bans and border policies.

She missed her family every day,
and told me what I do is enough,
that my presence made her feel safe,
and through my patience, she has felt love.
For indeed, the bonds of family transcend
miles, laws, and walls.

COVID Can't Stop Me

by Carol Grabowski

And I thought the Zika epidemic was bad! Testing, counseling, restricting travel. But all that was nothing compared to COVID-19.

In April, when COVID first hit our nation hard, I was out of the fray. I felt like a soldier observing a war rather than being down in the trenches fighting it. I'm a 67-year-old OB GYN in Southern California. There had been a decreased workload at our clinic when COVID outbreaks caused routine care to be put on hold, and I left the clinic so my Nurse Practitioner colleague could keep working.

I decided to volunteer with the Medical Reserve Corps. I was assigned to the COVID screening tent. In full PPE and sanitizer in ample supply, I vetted people who suspected they were infected. Indeed many were, and I sent them home. It felt good to be part of a national effort, all of us working together. Other dedicated volunteers included a retired aerospace engineer who oversaw sanitation of our workplace, and several National Guard corpsmen. I believed that we volunteers were reducing the medical staff's workloads.

Four months later, in August, after I had enjoyed lazy mornings in bed, reading and sipping my coffee, re-acquainting myself with my house, planning a remodel, COVID surged. I felt sure I was not ready to retire, so I returned to work part-time. I felt extreme concern for my medical colleagues, of all fields, being overwhelmed with the increase in infected patients. I worked from home for three-and-a-half days per week conducting telemedicine, and a half-day per week in the clinic.

A turning point came during three days in November when I returned more fully to the clinic as a substitute for the NP. Patients were all screened at the door, and nobody seemed symptomatic.

However, I developed a headache, nausea, and chills. I regurgitated at noon one cold, cloudy day and felt better. I felt shaky throughout my body and felt extra-anxious, unsurprisingly, with the pandemic surging as medical experts had warned with the coming of winter. My oxygen saturation was normal, but my pulse was rapid at rest, as I worked at home on my laptop. I wore a sweatshirt around the house, a rarity while dealing with menopausal hot flashes. I worried that I was infected and might die. As soon as I could, I got tested.

Three days later, my test result came back positive. I tried to get monoclonal antibodies, but my hospital wasn't set up for these infusions at that time. Fortunately, however, my symptoms remained mild, and my appetite and sense of smell soon returned. It was a tremendous relief to learn that by Day 6, COVID symptoms in most people have peaked, as was true in my case. I was grateful that I never went to ICU or needed a ventilator. But I remain cautious, foregoing my spontaneous weekend outings and still masking in indoor places. I consciously focus on what I *can* do rather than focusing always on what I *can't do.* It feels somewhat like PTSD.

Back in the clinic full-time now, I'm trying my best to convince our patients to get vaccinated against COVID. We long ago realized that logical explanations for vaccines have been given *ad infinitum* and that we must move beyond that stage. Now we focus on making direct, personal, heartfelt appeals to patients, hoping to influence them emotionally. Sadly but unavoidably, I have progressed from feeling frustrated to being furiously angry with those who refuse vaccines.

I constantly seek suggestions from other providers who are also trying their best to get patients vaccinated. This is a fight, a mission, we cannot abandon. I give myself a star for every successful "sales pitch" that closes the deal with a jab!

Sunset at Top of the World
... for Anne Grete

by Jane Hilary

From high we look down
to the quiet water
    stretching
        east — west
    grey as a dove's wing
—we know a body can fly like a bird —
    away
to the low, dark island
  back-lit in pink
    pale as a shell

Now you speak
of the death of your son

       — suicide
 — a body can fly like a bird —

So many came
   you were amazed.
So gentle a soul
  God is good
   you say

Driving down the mountain
all hell breaks loose —
Turquoise, like sea-glass
   bursts through the windshield

and clouds
scarlet as flame
flock toward heaven
beating in chorus
　　their glorious wings

Song for Healing
by Jane Hilary

Nothing but time
everything's humming
bees round the buds of the bent avocado
drone of a plane in a puff of ether
blue, blue burgeoning sky

Bees round the buds of the bent avocado
black wires bejeweled with murmuring birds
blue, so blue the burgeoning sky-way
Om Anandham Namah

Wires bejeweled with murmuring starlings
February sun cradles the teacup
Om Anandham Namah
Blessed this season of re-generation

February sun cradling the teacup
Esperanza, breeze through the palm fronds
blessed this season of regeneration
pain the fume of an ancient rhyme

Esperanza! Breeze through the palm fronds
brave choirs of angels summoning Spring
pain the fume of an archaic rhythm
lost in the thrum of the echoing sky

Choirs of daffodils summoning Springtime
drone of a plane in a puff of ether
wires of starlings whirring the mantra
Everything's humming
Nothing but time

Outside Therapy
by Lisa C. Krueger

Sitting across from someone closing
his eyes, I can't do this.

A canopy of oaks, ribbons, skin;
somewhere leaf-blowers drone.

Leaning toward one who weeps,
a lizard by her shoe.

Feathers from a hawk-ravaged nest
make a mandala on grass.

90 degrees. A woman says, I left, then
panicked, went back.

95 degrees. A man shouts,
I don't know who they want me to be!

Out in the open, gestures look theatrical,
on stage; a squirrel pauses.

Late afternoon, someone whispers,
I am always afraid.

Acorns, feathers, strips of shed skin,
bone bits and seed stipple: what was alive,

what wants to live. All day with trees,
grove of the unbroken.

Origami Night

by Lisa C. Krueger

Can't breathe, she says,
my chest hurts to inhale –

isolation flattens me.
My body folds into itself.

Breathe like this,
I say, slow ocean

sound of mouth,
air from my body

on the phone –
My head is light,

she whispers,
what if I pass out–

Breath is a raft,
I say; the phone

on my desk is dark –
little black box –

I catch my breath.
Twilight whisper
of a thousand cranes,
I hear her breathe –

I breathe –
we are breathing –

Saguaro Cacti

by Lisa C. Krueger

A medicine woman in Ojai
sings in Lakota
over my daughter's body

then informs me
it's my sickness
not my daughter's

I swear off healers
until Shaman John
famous for hard cases

of mothers like me
who are parched
as cacti out Route 66

He instructs my daughter
to lie on his bed
which smells of whiskey

then places crystals
on her chest
tells me to leave

my energy
is interfering
I step out to asphalt
that melts my flip-flops
rise up with the Saguaros
symbols of motherly love

Chronic

by Lisa C. Krueger

The body doesn't care how wealthy you are, or famous, or intelligent. The body has more power. Illness reminds us that we are beholden. No matter our level of fitness or personal determination, our depth of spiritual connection or self-affirmation, the body wins. Illness, that unwelcome guest, strips away the black belt. There are only so many moves to make when facing a fever. A failing heart. A lung that won't expand. A cell that won't stop mutating.

Twenty-five years ago, when I was a young psychologist and my daughter was four, she became ill with an array of debilitating symptoms that no one understood: lethargy, swollen glands, an enlarged spleen; wrists, ankles, knees that hurt. Stomach pain. Doctor's visits circled around everyone's private fear of cancer. Repeated blood tests, physical exams, appointments with specialists offered no clarity. No one talked about Dysautonomia, POTS, Ehler's Danlos, Mast Cell Activation Syndrome, or Chronic Undifferentiated Tissue Disease – diagnoses that would be confirmed a decade later. Instead, doctors and educators talked to us about tolerance. The importance of resting, then getting back out in the world.

"How bad is the sore throat, really?" one teacher inquired. The administrator of her school told me my daughter was probably just depressed. Our pediatrician informed me he suspected an ulcer, and that he was sure my husband and I were putting too much pressure on her. A friend took me to lunch to tell me, "You should consider boarding school in the future. It would be good for her, and for you."

Illness is something every parent searches for and hopes never to find. Yet we always do, at some juncture of the journey—the flushed face, the fever in the night, the listless body. Is our baby alright? Our child? Our teen? It can't be too serious, right? It has to pass, right?

Carry on. Health, for many—if they are lucky—feels like a right. An entitled wealth, even. Illness, then, can seem an aberration.

A mistake. I have noticed that people often feel sorry for the sick child: the first grader who misses a week of school for the flu, the high schooler with mono who can't go to prom. But the chronically ill child elicits different feelings. This child alludes to life's mysteries, the larger powers of nature or god or circumstance—depending on personal belief—that we can't comprehend or control. The ill child reminds us of what doesn't blend in with the lights and glitter of yearning and hope. The ill child reminds us of darkness.

Throughout my years of work as a therapist, I have been deeply affected by the isolation of illness. How often people who endure some of the most painful experiences in life—depression, panic, phobia, paranoia—feel completely alone in their suffering. Connection and community are necessary to healing. Yet we abandon one other.

The pandemic has opened my heart even wider to the ways in which we suffer. People have sought therapy for problems they never expected to encounter: issues related to family, friends, and community, questions about personal identity or sense of self that had never arisen before COVID. The current global health crisis has required many to rethink beliefs and life choices. Most significantly in my therapy practice, the pandemic has eroded a fundamental resilience that many took for granted, leaving them feeling less capable, often less hopeful, about their future.

Today, many of my daughter's health challenges from Dysautonomia resemble those of COVID long-haulers. Exhaustion. Tachycardia. Joint pain. Sleep issues. Digestion issues. Brain fog.

Her brain fog is my nemesis. I can hardly bear it, some days, how suddenly she can't think straight or speak clearly, or at all. Brain scans show a sixty-two percent reduction in cerebral blood flow for her when she has just a mild episode of syncope, meaning there is barely enough oxygen going to the brain. We might be cooking together, or driving on an errand, or just sitting, and one of many triggers will elicit a change. Her autonomic nervous system is exquisitely sensitive. Sometimes I think of it like a finely tuned, specialized race car. One minute my daughter is here, in this life: thinking, feeling, articulating her amazing self. Then she is gone. As though she left, all of a sudden, on an unexpected trip. Persephone.

One of the things I admire most about my daughter is what I think of as her philosophy of endurance. Sometimes she is so ill that she is barely conscious. Then her body finds its way back; she picks up where she left off and goes on. I think of her as a tree in the wind. She bends but does not break. Keeps growing.

My daughter spends much of her life alone: resting, recovering, gathering strength to be in the world, as health allows. She is an incredible artist and writer. She helped create a support network for people with POTS and has a wonderful online community of friends. "Together, alone," she says to me about her life.

There is so much to come that we can't predict. The pandemic world is filled with change and uncertainty. My daughter has learned to navigate the pitfalls and pain of life with an attitude of grit and expectation: she gets through difficult episodes to anticipate better times.

I wish for everyone that health challenges and life challenges might open doors to new ways of seeing and being. I wish that COVID might connect all of us to a larger purpose . . . and to each other.

Friendship as practiced by Jean

by Alexandra M. Levine

The Covid came on strong
And stayed a long while
More than 5 weeks already
No appetite
But that didn't matter
Couldn't get out of bed, let alone cook

Then came Jean
Bringing homemade soups
Vegetable, bean, onion, minestrone
With meatballs
Her daughter made gallons of bone broth
10 grams of protein in every cup
Then, home-baked coffee cakes
Banana, apple and cinnamon pecan
Followed by spaghetti with sauce
And more meatballs
Bags of potatoes and oranges
Apples and melons
Crackers and breads
And so much more

Driving up to the top of the driveway
Placing her boxes on the concrete

And walking away

After mutual blowing of kisses and hugs
Given across the window glass
She, back to her kitchen
Me, back to my bed
Friendship expressed in this way
Suffused with love and care
How lucky I am

My Healing Anodyne

by Frank L. Meyskens, Jr.

Healing is an ancient art
long practiced around the fireside
in times of disease and damage,
from whatever the cause therein.

And we moderns find a way
to enlightenment as science unveils
secrets that underlie causality,
leading to drugs and other potions.

As the healer in the white coat
builds trust that enables me
to be probed and prodded,
my corporeal being aching.

But when the moment became dire
your hands covered mine and
I feel you once again, my loving anodyne.
Hope restored and healing begins again.

Connections

by Frank L. Meyskens, Jr.

Hugging, a universal gesture.
When done well,
like holding hands with your whole body.
When done with malintent,
like a punch to the gut.

There is an infinite variety of hugs:

There is the business hug,
brief arm contact around one shoulder,
a greeting familiar to all, saying,
    "I'm here."
      But nothing more.

There is the faithful colleague hug,
arms encircling each other,
bodies facing and apart,
accompanied by a smile,
and a brief meeting of the eyes.

And then, the good friend hug.
A brief contact of bodies
    with a felt response,
a peck on the cheek,
    a slow parting of the flesh.

And unexpectedly, moments that we all remember.
Two bodies
    entangled from head to toe,
leaving nothing
  to the imagination.

And hands.
Two people gently holding hands while walking down the street.
The caregiver, softly touching the hand
    of a patient or a loved one,
  signaling kindness and love,
      building empathy and trust.

Hugging and holding hands.
Two ancient forms of communication.
Transmitting compassion and understanding.
Keeping peace, building healing and hope.

    Nurturing, fostering, connecting....
      the chance for another day.

Abscopal Outcomes

by Frank L. Meyskens, Jr.

Reflections on Distant Effects,
the abscopal effect, called nonsensical
when I was in medical school fifty years ago.
Now being hailed as the explanation for
distant outcomes far from the radiation site.
Complex molecular and chemical signaling
resulting in away-from-primary target responses,
molecular injury, the cellular Lyft for rides
to unsuspected places.

But why should abscopal seem so foreign
while, in the quantum world,
Schrödinger's cat lives in two boxes simultaneously.
And every morning, both a particle with mass
and a wave which has none,
illuminating our world, stretching our disbelief
about what we think and know.

And so on to those moments when
at the end-of-life the light begins to fade,
respondent to heroics
but seemingly hopeless
when the therapies have been many.

But unlike the day, the night begins
in light as if from further away,
creating hopefulness when there was none.
The right cell responding to a distant star,

striking down the malignant counterpart.
And are the physical and biological
worlds so different, both with
classical continuous and quantum discontinuous events?
Who knows, when it seems like every day
新 new universes are being discovered far away
and only one of several hundred passengers
survives a fiery crash, untouched.

So don't tell me that something is nonsense...impossible.
The true creative moment that leads to deep understanding
is always a distant star, far ahead of the wave
that generates innovation, outcomes, and hopefulness,
illuminating understanding of the heart and soul of this walking,
talking primate by the warmth of the fireside.

Originally published in a prior version in *Practical Radiation Oncology* (Sept-Oct., 2019), p. 294, PMID 31103714.
A podcast discussing the origin of this poem can be Googled at "Practical Radiation Oncology podcast Meyskens."

The Newspeak Mask

by Frank L. Meyskens, Jr.

Now your mask protects me
from death transmitted in the air.
Eyes playing hide-and-seek
with emotions.
Tonal melodies communicating
the mood of the moment.

No touching in this new world.
Hugs condemned to virtuality.
We become muggers of empathy,
 obliterating kindness and compassion.

Now my mask shields me
from digital algorithms on the hunt,
searching for identities to condemn
each one of us as we enter

an Orwellian tomorrow.

Love in the Time of COVID-19
...a pantoum
by Gabriella Miotto

Now that you are not allowed to touch me
I want to be sheltered by the language of the birds
and a thundering Buffalo drum
heart of one who returned from near-extinction.

[handwritten: PROTECTIVE CLOTHING WORN BY DR. IN A PLAGUE]

I want to be sheltered by the language of the birds
while *il medico della peste* wears an N95 this time around
and the heart of one who returned from near-extinction
watches us make green pesto and music for one another

while *il medico della peste* wears an N95 this time   *[handwritten: REMEMBER YOU MUST DIE]*
not smelling of lavender and mint but *memento mori* still,
and watches us make green pesto and music for one another
even though potato bins are empty and paper hoarded

not smelling of lavender and mint but still *memento mori*
we rage instead at death, block the reaper's entrance
even though potato bins are empty and paper hoarded
and dolphins return to Molo Audace and skies reclaim their blue
     [handwritten: STONE PIER IN TRIESTE, IT]

and we laugh at death, block the reaper's entrance
hear a thundering Buffalo drum
as dolphins return to Molo Audace and skies reclaim their blue
now that I am not allowed to touch you.

49

Daimon
by Gabriella Miotto

Census and censer sound so similar
  but one is for counting the living
    the other for claiming   our dead

and as our conversation ends you tell me
  frankly   you want to be numbered among the survivors
    not carried with incense to the land of   ghosts

want to be like the yellow daffodil
  who   unflinching in its gaze
    stares   in the face
        grey winter.

Death and beauty share the same table
always every day sometimes sitting   6 feet apart
sometimes
       in each other's laps.

I wake from a dream of suffocation
no   mask or ventilator in sight
ask the wind to clear   fear from my face and voice

and walk outside to watch bees search for nectar
  hovering
      above the red freesia
    focused on the honey-making.

Salami Is Your Talisman
...for my parents

by Gabriella Miotto

The word arises during an Italian lunch
of yeasted bread and mortadella we share
across the metal screen of your bedroom window
mask removed, you indoors, me outdoors.
Thank God you're on the first floor
not hovering on a second or 13th.

You want salami next time.

It penetrates your ritual afternoon nap
and you are temporarily healed
by this dish, with its salt
now streaming down face as tears,
calling out to your long-dead friend Carlo
provider of fermented meats and cheeses
and conversations that cure loneliness.

And perhaps he is here again with you
as you try to rise from bed to greet him
strong in that moment, leg and shoulder
unfettered by fracture and fear,
warmed by this cold cut made for times
of meager portions.

You put face and hands against the window
and I become a palm reader.

The Territory
by Gabriella Miotto

I've been wandering the grounds of this homestead
looking for the animal that keeps scratching at my windows and
doors.

Some days it seems beaked, others, clawed.
Perhaps an injured bird, feathers askew in the aftermath of feline
jaws?

> *I want to warm you gently in my palms, reset your wings.*

Or perhaps a wolf, bloodied paws still harnessed to the steel trap?

> *I want to bandage your wounds, offer your limbs deliverance.*

What?
You say those sounds of screeching tapping whimpering scratching
   are coming from me?

Well then.

Will you help me
   tend to my song and my flight
      to my howl and my hunt?

And I will, yours.

Mask
by Stacy Nigliazzo

My borrowed face

                     incorporeal,   blue—

I give you   only

                   my eyes.

Apex, Pandemic I

by Stacy Nigliazzo

He arrives choke-winded,   vespid breath

     like pollen on a windshield.

I am the first one—

     I steady my gloved hand across his chest.

His heart is an angry fist.

     We place a breathing tube.

I step back and hold my breath.

     His lungs   bloom,

        hands   open

        like sunflowers.

Carillon

by Stacy Nigliazzo

I call to tell him she is   *here,*

         and *not here;*

     that her heart   stopped,

            then started again,

   and we are seeking her in every lampblack corridor.

And when I hold the phone to her ear

       so he can read to her,

           her

        eyes

             ring—

When they ask how he died I tell them
by Stacy Nigliazzo

he found the gate unlatched,

        crossed the downy path

      into the volant field,

pressed his palm against a river birch carved with his name,

     his breath, a brace of stars —

        and never looked back.

Heart as an esker

by Kathleen Powers

I.

There was once a river
Where fingers now are

A whole flood
And now we're in it.

II.

The strange thing about thinking is that
It possesses no force.

As he held the heart in his hands
The edges kept caving in.

I kept putting them back
Putting
Them
Back
As if to preserve their form would mean something.

III.

Meaning in an ancient riverbed arrives as the water and
Seafoamed life you'd imagined there
Dissipate

And you're on the banks as you always were
Marooned
(An observer's status is always a marooned one)
Not realizing you're in it.

That's you, dear.
The khaki-ed paleontologist of the anatomy lab.
Enclosed in sedimentary fascia
Looking at something else
The earth has poured itself over.

IV.

You are both on and beside the table.
The carapace is formaldehyde.
You plug a valve with your thumb.

V.

The day you zoomed about necrosis
You saw a wall of cinderblocks
As a dike freshly lain
Across what used to be the library.

You ask the foreman:
"What..."
He replies:
"Labs."

Knowledge and life are at odds with each other.
But you knew that before
Seeing forms in the basalt and limestone.

You shrug. Aristotle said 'like attracts like.'
And you went out looking for fossils.

Minneapolis Burning

by Chalat Rajaram

Knee on neck as life leaves,
Pleading yet the cry unheard,
Striking at the core of beliefs,
Of human dignity lost, as feared.

Too slow to call out injustice,
People taking to the street.
In such a moment this pandemic,
The stopping of a heartbeat.

Pleas in Navajo, Spanish, English
Tears and grief, this gnawing deep.
Wherefore we headed, is there a wish,
Is there a soul, why can't we weep?

The launch of dragon rocket today
Brings pride and joyful celebration.
US-built launched this end of May,
A smile amidst this deep depression.

Over a hundred-thousand dead this year,
The country reeling, far from healing,
Impatience bursting, hard to bear,
As Minneapolis is burning.

Loss
by Chalat Rajaram

Did we not lose hundreds of thousands?
Nay, millions of bodies, to this pandemic
Across our vast globe, bodies of all
Ages, caste, creed, color --
Bodies with ideas, thoughts, aspirations,
Suffering, gone in a whiff with
Bad decisions, misinformation
Innocent or willful,
Ill-prepared, naïve,
Ego-filled, selfish hearts --
Where was empathy?
While millions of these souls left their bodies
On further journeys unknown.

Travel inwards to be better
For others and ourselves.
In countries across this globe,
Times call for a change in approach
Early in life to care, find the Self,
And see others, ourselves differently
As one.

Blessing
by Chalat Rajaram

A fresh hope, a bright new day
Prayers last night, family and friend
Feel so blessed, waking today
But when will these COVID times end?

Then the roses burst from buds
In front gardens and backyard
With sun breaking through the clouds
Time to let go, drop my guard.

Hard times have not ended
However, while a lot better here
In India, life seems upended
Prayers for health, easing the fear.

Deaths of millions, grief, sadness
The soul never dies, never they say
Prayers, thoughts, faithfulness
Efforts to feel deep, to find a way.

Mini-Chronicle of a Pandemic: A Sestina

by Jose L. Recio

If one stays at home
going out only to walk the dog
and safely do a few errands in the neighborhood,
the worry about the ongoing pandemic
caused by the new coronavirus can be more bearable,
especially if one learns to filter the swarming news in the media.

Yet it is hard today to limit connections with the media
or disconnect ourselves from others and stay home.
We do it faithfully till the burden makes it unbearable.
To complicate matters, this pandemic might even affect dogs.
The world is unprepared to deal with this pandemic,
a fact acknowledged in most neighborhoods.

But "I don't want that to happen in my neighborhood"
doesn't apply here even when protests clog the media.
In medieval times, these events were "acts of God," but now a
        pandemic,
caused by a virus, requiring people to stay home,
and not go out unless it's safe or only to walk the dog.
To develop patience will be a gift making the burden more
        bearable.

But in reality, the rules remain unbearable.
"I'm bored to death," some say, at least in my neighborhood,
And we feel propelled to do something, but the best thing is
        walking the dog.
Many suggestions and fears are spread through the media,
with aims of "flattening the curve," which starts at home.
Each country develops different ways to fight this pandemic.

Coronavirus emerged in China and soon grew into a pandemic:
crossing borders, destined to become unbearable,
even before we were told to stay at home:
"If you go out, just stroll on the streets in your neighborhood."
Understandably, people clung to their phone, TV, and so on—the
        media—
people avoiding one another, staying closer to their dogs.

Pets seem safe for now, but let's keep an eye on it, for dogs
are beginning to be tested, and it's not clear they're immune to this
        pandemic.
News become overwhelming and scary, but we all depend on the
        media
to make sense of the events, share, and make life a bit more
        bearable,
and, above all, to remain on good terms with the neighborhood,
even if only communicating by texting and email from home.

We stay home to stop the pandemic from spreading,
Keep up with the media and go out to walk the dog.
All measures to make the crisis more bearable in our neighborhood.

In Need of a Prayer

by Jo Marie Reilly

The new patient's name is Emmanuel. He was sent from his nursing home to our emergency room with a cough and fever. The oxygen level in his blood is well below normal, and he's gasping for air.

It's my third week in the local community hospital ER. I've been putting in extra on-call time during the COVID pandemic. It's been rough to get back into the emergency setting while continuing my day job as a family doctor and medical educator. I've been sharing admissions with the hospitalist, who's joined me in the on-call room.

"I'll take him," I tell my colleague.

"Sure?" he asks, eyebrows arched over his face mask.

The pager blares again.

I nod, then dash down the hallway.

Lubing up with hand sanitizer for what seems the hundredth time today, I grab gloves, gown and cap and don my N-95 mask, goggles and face shield.

Preparing to enter the patient's room, I stop and squint at a document I hadn't seen before on the door:

COVID SUSPECT ROOM OCCUPATION
How many minutes were you in the room?
Did you have on an N-95 mask?
Did the patient have on a mask?
Did you use the medical equipment in the room or your own?

I mentally check off each one, marveling at how complex it's become to conduct a medical history, physical exam, and clinical assessment.

Opening the door, I'm struck by the deafening roar of the mechanical-ventilation system. *How in the world can I expect to hear his lungs through the stethoscope?* I think, and then, *Does it even matter?*

Catching my first glimpse of Emmanuel, I'm overwhelmed with a sense of futility. Does he stand a chance of making it through this vicious virus? His bloated belly protrudes grandly from his 300-plus-pound frame. His legs are the size of the oak trees lining the streets around my home. His oxygen mask is slipping off his face.

With a deep sigh, I pull it together to give him the best I've got. Instinctively, I reach out and return the mask straps to their proper position behind his ears.

Oops! Am I supposed to do that?

Despite the mask, Emmanuel is struggling to breathe, his chest muscles tugging fiercely over his rib cage.

"You hanging in there?" I ask. "What can I do to help?"

"I just can't keep this mask on my face!" Agitatedly, he twists it behind his ears.

I put my stethoscope against his scorching-hot skin and strain to hear his lung sounds. Completing his exam, I note his mental clarity—a rarity among the nursing-home patients I've been admitting.

"Do you have family members I can be in touch with, to let them know you're in the hospital?" I ask.

"My wife will only be terrified," he confesses. "She hated me going to the convalescent center, but she couldn't care for me at home. My cell phone will die soon, and I don't have a charger. No way to tell her myself."

I shake my head at how isolated hospitalized patients are now. Amid the pandemic, cell phones have been a gift to most of us, yet when patients get admitted to the hospital, no one tells them to bring in a cell-phone cord. They're swallowed up within the medical system; no family member can see them, and few can contact them.

I pause. My next question is a very painful and difficult one.

"We're asking all of our patients what their wishes may be should their hearts stop beating, or should they stop breathing," I say gently.

"I've lived a good long life," he says. "If it's my time, it's my time." His voice fades, but above his mask, his eyes are clear and piercing.

I realize that the minutes are ticking away. I remember the sign on Emmanuel's door, demanding that I chart the time I'm here with him. Each minute puts me and my family and elderly parents at progressively greater risk, but I need to help him through this delicate and important conversation about his end-of-life needs.

I think of my own father—so fragile, admitted to the hospital three times in the last five months. If he were here, I think, I'd certainly want his physician to have this discussion with him. The thought hits too close to home, so I push it aside.

Sitting a safe distance from Emmanuel, I summon my most caring tone of voice to deliver pointed questions about how to direct his medical care if he stops breathing. I keep glancing at my watch, feeling an increasingly urgent need to leave the room.

On my way out, I pause and rest my hand on Emmanuel's shoulder. "We will do our best to care for you," I say.

Outside, I peel off my COVID gear and scrub my goggles and hands with disinfectant wipes.

∞

In the ER, the attending doc shouts to no one in particular: "Code blue in room 16! Didn't make it."

This patient arrived in full cardiac arrest, then died, despite the team's best efforts. My colleague's pain is palpable, but there's no time to process the loss; I hurry to my next patient.

66

Dwayne is tremulous and detoxing, his heart racing. Slurring his words and picking at his hospital gown, he tells me how he lost his job last week due to COVID layoffs. Feeling panicked and cut off from the support of his Alcoholics Anonymous community, he went on a vodka bender.

My thoughts turn to Veronica, who visited my clinic two days ago, right after suffering a miscarriage. She carried her eight-week-old baby (too small for a mortuary cremation) in a Tupperware baggie.

"If I went to the ER," she confided, "I'm afraid the nurses would flush my baby down the toilet."

COVID has deprived her of the presence of family, friends and her spiritual community, who could give her the support she craves while grieving her lost hope for a child. She handed me the baggie, and I mustered some words of comfort, keenly aware that she needed more.

Veronica and Dwayne are just two instances of how COVID has impacted patients' day-to-day lives, preying on the most vulnerable.

∞

Trudging out of the hospital at 1:30 a.m., I whisk off my mask, grateful to breathe in the fresh night air and rub my ears, aching from being squeezed beneath the tight mask strings for eight hours straight. My hands smell of the bleach wipes with which I incessantly wipe down my cell phone, stethoscope and computer, even in the "safety" of the doctors' call room.

Being a doctor takes its toll. I'm grateful to sit quietly in the car for a few minutes, my COVID clothes and shoes stashed safely in a Hefty trash bag. I reflect on the ER shift, the madness, the intensity of pain and illness, the Band-Aiding I did with each patient. It never felt quite adequate. I remember Veronica and others like her, hurting and in desperate need of caring and compassion.

Feeling physically and emotionally exhausted, I drive home with Celine Dion and Andrea Bocelli's "The Prayer" blaring. Its final lines keep replaying in my mind, echoing my own prayer for healing and strength:

When we lose our way
Lead us to a place
Guide us with your grace
Give us faith so we'll be safe....

Originally published in *Pulse » In Need of a Prayer,* by PulseVoices.org, on 8/23/21.
https://pulsevoices.org/index.php/stories/in-need-of-a-prayer/print/

I Lost My Sister to COVID

by Lorna Rodríguez-Rodríguez

I am a surgeon and in a senior leadership position at a major medical center, so when I look back at all the turmoil that was going on at work, in the country, and around the world at the beginning of the COVID pandemic, what I was going through was turbulent and happening so fast, I didn't have time to reflect. Now it's time to begin to deal with what I, and many others, experienced.

In April and May of 2020, I was extremely busy clinically because our team decided that the doctors in the division with small children should stay home; and the ones, like me, with grown kids would be on call more often. We also didn't know what to do for self-protection from the virus. There was just so little information available. We focused on protecting the patients the best we could, but without testing or any real understanding, at the time, of the modes of contagion, we were operating blindfolded.

I was actually on call every day for two weeks in a row – and during all that time I was sure I was going to get COVID. Between my allergies and being Latinx, and the number of hours on call and in harm's way, I knew I was at a much higher risk of a severe disease and even death. It was exhausting and a bit surreal, but it all turned so much worse when it became clear to me what indeed eventually happened…that my sister was going to die.

My beloved sister, who was also a doctor, was living in Spain and was caring for a dear friend hospitalized with COVID. When we spoke as the days passed, my sister sounded congested, then she developed a high fever, then she lost her appetite, then she had a terrible sore throat, and finally she got out of breath just taking a shower. She got tested for COVID and was immediately admitted into the ICU.

69

I talked to her every day while she could and then... no more communication. It was terrifying.

The constant uncertainty of not knowing what was happening, combined with the time zone differences, meant that I would wake up several times during the night to look at the phone and make sure I hadn't missed a call. My friends in Spain, bless their hearts, often didn't keep track of the time difference so they would call whenever there was news. The feeling of constant helplessness was overwhelming. I also had this powerful feeling that I was failing my sister, who had always been there for me.

A few words about my sister, Raquel Emilia Rodríguez Rodríguez: She was a neuroscientist, with a PhD in physical chemistry. She developed a passion for understanding human diseases and taught at the Medical School at the University of Salamanca, and the University of Avila, both in Spain. My sister stood only 4' 11" tall, but this tiny woman had a giant heart with love that poured out of her effortlessly. She was beloved by her students, who numbered in the thousands over the years. She was also an internationally known and respected scientist. She was the first one to clone the pain receptor genes in zebra fish. My sister was one of those people who always went well beyond the call of duty in everything she did. Now she needed help, but I could do *nothing*! I could only wait for news, then relay what I learned to the rest of our family.

The last time I spoke with Raquel on Zoom, she had become so short of breath, that I could see her abdomen undulating up and down. I knew her abdominal muscles were working hard to push the lungs up because the diaphragm movement was not enough for sufficient oxygen exchange. I have that moment imprinted in my brain.

I got so scared, I didn't want her to talk anymore in case she got even more short of breath, so I told her, let's hang up so you can

70

rest. We will talk later.

Later never happened.

I found an old student of hers who is now a doctor and asked him to check on her. His email to me was so full of pain. He had to tell me there was no hope. She was going from organ failure to organ failure.

I kept wondering if I had thought of calling him sooner, could he have made a difference? His email caused me a sudden grief that was piercing and intense, so intense that it numbed my body and yet left my mind completely clear, with an undeniable perfect knowledge of what was happening and what was to come.

After four long days, the awful message telling me it was over came in. It arrived in the middle of the night, so I got up and took a long shower so that my oldest son, who was in the bedroom next to mine, couldn't hear me cry. I dressed and went to the hospital to make rounds, but once I got there, I locked myself in my office and wept until I was out of breath. Then I sat there doing nothing, feeling nothing, thinking nothing.

As awful as all that is to remember, I do have one story that I hold on to. There was a doctor from another town at the hospital that day. She didn't know my sister, but she heard all the daily commotion in her room – all my sister's students, now friends, visiting her – and she got curious and went to meet her. She later told me that she had never seen someone die with such grace and peace as my sister did. She also shared that Raquel was never left alone; most of those students she taught were now her doctors and cared for her and loved her. They held her hand, and they gave her love, until the end.

And now I want to meet them. I want to hold their hands and give them my loving thanks for being there when I could not.

Preventing Scarring of the Soul
by Lorna Rodriguez-Rodriguez

The major social and behavioral changes our world experienced with the coronavirus pandemic in 2020, and continues to grapple with, were inevitable. In the healthcare field, things got complicated and too dynamic very swiftly, with changes in rules and treatments happening sometimes by the hour.

When my sister Raquel, a medical scientist, risked her life to care daily for her COVID-stricken friend, the hospital in which she worked in Spain did not have proper PPE, because most of the world did not know enough about how to deal with the novel virus at the time. While my surgical team and I eventually had enough PPE in the United States, my sister and her fellow medical staff had to make their own face shields out of plastic sheets they carried in their binders. As dire as it was here, the contrast in the ability of each country to respond and adjust to the daily input of knowledge was humbling.

Until the day I got Raquel's death certificate, eight months after her demise, I was in denial. Actually, I was numb; I am still numb. But I had to become a phoenix. I packed down my pain and once again rose from the ashes and got back to work, focusing on social justice and how to vaccinate more people of color and how to decrease the health inequities in this country and hopefully globally. My sister would be so happy to know I am not crying anymore and that I instead choose to be a change agent so that fewer families experience last good-byes, or as in my case, no goodbyes at all.

As I continued to work long hours, I eventually stepped back into my body and tried to heal my aching spirit. Amazingly, it doesn't matter how much you push your feelings down into a compact little box, grief sneaks out, with unexpected timing and with unnerving intensity.

What made the entire inevitable process harder was that even in a healthcare setting, people don't like to witness grief. It's true that most people around me didn't know what I was going through, but even those who did tended to look away or forget. Fortunately, I have one friend that often asks: "So, how is your grieving coming along?" The question is so direct, and he asks it bravely with the knowledge that I am not done grieving. I wonder if anyone ever is.

He tells me that grief is different for everyone, but that it has frequency, duration, and intensity. I think of it like sound waves. The frequency will go down, so that I don't think about it every day anymore; the duration will get shorter, so I will be struck by this piercing hurt, but it will last minutes now instead of a whole day. But, and here is the hardest part, the intensity does not change, and I wonder if it ever will.

But this story is not only about death and grief in the middle of a pandemic and social turmoil. This is also a story about how health care workers have developed a culture where others go first, even if we are melting inside from grief, burnout, and pure exhaustion. I still try to make sense of why I didn't take time off to heal, why I didn't ask a colleague to take my call on that awful day, why I took care of patients that needed all of my attention when I had none left to give.

I was watching a special recently about Naomi Osaka, the tennis champion, and her coach said that she needed to learn to play her best even when that day her best was not 100%. That is what we do as health care providers: we learn to function even if we are not 100%.

We master how to perform surgery with precision even when we're feeling sick, and how to prescribe medications with accurate dosages even when we're sleepy, how to push our bodies farther

73

than our minds can. And we do our very best not to hurt anyone (but ourselves) in the process.

During the pandemic, as some of our team got physically ill, and members of the extended staff could not come to work, there were fewer and fewer of us able bodies available to take care of the patients. We needed to put our souls in a prolonged pause so that we could keep caring for others and yet do no harm.

Years of training allowed that to happen, almost smoothly. And yet, many physicians and health care workers did die by suicide during this time. Pushing ourselves to the limit does have consequences, some visible and some invisible.

I know that when you are in a war, as we were, and to this day still are, you can't stop for each wounded fellow soldier in the field. You need to keep moving forward for the good of the majority. When the battle is over, then you can address your grieving and hopefully start to heal your soul. *I also know that if you don't start your healing process in a timely fashion, those soul wounds become scars, and scars on the soul decrease flexibility, empathy, patience, joy.*

I think I was able to address my grief in time, but not all of us were that fortunate. So now I ask: How can we balance that ingrained sense of duty that is part of our medical culture—that capacity we develop to do unthinkable things with our bodies and minds—with self-care? How can we balance that and not develop the scars that can never be healed? Is it possible?

And perhaps more importantly, can we help each other along the way? Can we stop in the middle of the battle and ask the wounded soldier: "How is your grieving going?"

Lately, I have been paying attention to the younger athletes, like Osaka and Simone Biles, who seem to be seeking answers to similar questions in their field. I am also listening to veterans in the medical community who have struggled for years with these predicaments. Maybe together we might find solutions faster.

74

When we give people who are in survival mode a voice and a time to vent, on a regular basis, by asking them thoughtful questions and really taking time to listen to their answers, that may slow down the development of the soul scars that can leave permanent damage.

Finally, my biggest hope is that you, the reader, can come up with better ideas...and that this story inspires you to publish them. I hope that you take the time now to face what you've been postponing. Reach out for help to those around you, and give yourself the time to take a breath, put yourself first, and truly grieve. That is the very best way we can honor those, like Raquel, whose lives we've lost but whom we will never stop loving and missing every day.

Uncle Lenny

by Steven T. Rosen

He taught me to spit, wipe drip from
my nose, swallow scotch with one gulp.
Drove that truck like a limousine, owned the road,
greeted the bums like they were generals.
Couldn't tell if here, in fantasy, reflection
or a tomorrow's moment.
Pot belly, soulful laugh, sway baby sway,
hug all those girls.
My uncle, my man, yes my man,
Took no shit, dignified sweatshirts, save your opinion.
All got respect, color no issue, wealth no issue.
He's gone, tender words, real tears, real love.
With his death some direction, with his death some comfort,
with his death I am freed.

COVID-19 Sequence

by Steven T. Rosen

1.

An insidious fog blankets the planet
Siphoning life from every shrub
Aligned with the wind sans boundaries
Lurking as a shadow filling each sinister crevice
Cryptic origin absent lucid culmination
We patiently wait knowing the only certainty is
That our love will endure

2.

Time has lost its cadence
Days blend without an apparent tomorrow
Oppressive gloom hovers suffocating joy
Finite or eternal torment
Speculation more concrete than fact
Future now an obscure journey

3.

Do we wake from hibernation
To a world abandoned by time and disease
Searching for answers only to discover questions
With lingering doubts of the process
Weighing the balance of isolation versus natural bonding
Hoping humanity will emerge with limited scars
Praying for resolution that leaves the essence of life intact

Originally appeared in a prior version in the author's poetry collection, *Heartfelt Reflections* (KDP, 2021).

My Nurse
by Steven T. Rosen

Beauty and eloquence hidden behind the ritual pandemic mask

Soft, mysterious eyes speak to a lifetime of empathy

Attentive to every detail executed with memorable precision

Possessing knowledge and skills honed through years of toil

Exemplifies service, compassion, and dedication to excellence

Cherished partner for lucky physicians

Blessing for a legion of patients

Originally appeared in a prior version in the author's poetry collection, *Heartfelt Reflections* (KDP, 2021).

The End?

by Steven T. Rosen

If I have another chance to say goodbye

It would not be the ICU

Hopefully time will be my ally

You will find the strength to heal

Let this not be my one great regret

Watching you silently pass in the night

You more than anyone

Deserve to hear I love you

One more time.

Originally appeared in a prior version in the author's poetry collection, *Heartfelt Reflections* (KDP, 2021).

Emerging During the Pandemic
by Johanna Shapiro

During the past seven months of quarantine in the coronavirus pandemic, I practically go nowhere except to my doctors and dentist. My only walking is around our neighborhood. At the end of the long, meandering street is a dead-end with a vista of hills and a vast, uncluttered sky.

When I reach this point, I raise my arms wide and utter the following prayer: "Protect Your servants. Help Your people. Save Your world." (Over the course of history, the Lord's servants have been a motley crew. For this reason, I want to clarify that, for the purposes of this prayer, I am referring to the essential workers and frontline doctors and nurses battling COVID-19).

I recite this prayer three times, each time separated by a respectful pause, which is inevitably met with silence . . . but it might be a Divine Silence, which could be replete with answers. Who knows what anything really means these days?

Then I turn around and go home. Usually I am able to indulge this practice in complete isolation because, although there are houses nearby, their inhabitants never emerge. Today, however, a middle-aged man materialized, heading toward his car. When he saw me, arms outstretched, he stood gawking at me like I was a crazy woman. He seemed eager to just drive away, but was perhaps worried I might attack his house . . . or more likely, curse it.

"What are you doing there?" he shouted at me.

"Praying," I replied calmly.

It took him a moment to process this. There was no church, mosque, or synagogue in sight. No choir, no prayer books, and as far as either of us could tell, no God.

He took a deep breath, looked quizzical, then slowly nodded and said, "Oh well then, that's all right. Go right ahead." He zoomed away, both of us waving farewell.

I finished my final round of supplications and walked home, smiling. Prayer never felt so neighborly . . . or maybe neighborliness never felt so prayerful.

Who knows what anything really means these days?

Dear Future (if you are still there)
by Johanna Shapiro

2020 was quite a year
Pandemic, quarantines
lockdowns
a crazy President
telling us not to worry
There was no pandemic
Inject bleach
Demonstrations against masks
"They stifle my freedom!"
(to be an idiot)
Doctors, nurses risking their lives
and their families' lives
fighting daily with few weapons
just their oath to heal
at least to care always
Hundreds of thousands of deaths
disproportionately among
people of color
a tsunami of suffering

Yes, 2020 was quite a year
(Yet another) awakening
to the endemic racism
of our country
Black Lives Matter
demonstrations in the streets
Finally, people of all colors
no longer afraid to recognize
Black and Brown injustice
countered by white supremacists
and neo-Nazis
no longer afraid to

show their ugly khakis and
Tiki torches
unafraid to shout their
ugly ideology

And of course there was still
climate change
continuing to smack us in the face
while we pretended
Mother Earth was not sick
        -- and sick of us
Fires, floods, hurricanes
heat waves, downpours
melting polar icecaps
rising sea levels
while governments dithered
and asserted something
must be done

2021 was supposed to be
better
We had vaccines
We had masks
We had a new President
whose trademark was empathy
We had learned some things about
crowds
unventilated spaces
testing
Or had we?
We rushed to reclaim our old lives
heedless of warnings of new variants
heedless of the hordes who
refused vaccination, refused masks,
preferred risking illness and
death
for themselves and

everyone around them
Delta struck
and now it was not just
(at times seemingly expendable)
old people and sick people
but younger folk
even kids in ICUs
Still we partied on
It was summer after all

Dear Future,
please write back and
tell me what happens
Are we caught in an endless loop of
more variants, more deaths,
more vaccines that people won't take
more denial, more politics?
Will we ever learn to do
the right thing?
Will we ever learn that
the virus doesn't care
if we are white, Black, Brown
what our politics are?
Will we ever learn that this is an
existential struggle?
If we don't come together
we will die separately
alone in overcrowded hospitals
and when they are too full
in parking lot tents

Did we ever figure this out,
dear Future?

In the Waiting Room
by Johanna Shapiro

In the waiting room
people pretend to look at their smart phones
shush their kids
ruffle ancient magazines
glare at the receptionist
when they think she can't see them

Really they are waiting --
to find out what's wrong
to find out what will fix them
Really they are waiting
for hope
or the pretense of hope

As for the doctors
behind the closed doors of their offices
they bang silently on their computers
They too are waiting --
for the day to end
so that they can stop

producing diagnoses
writing prescriptions
arguing insurance
listening to too many stories
offering hope
or the pretense of hope

So that they can finally go home
where they pretend to check their phones,
shush their kids
answer their emails
gaze at their spouses
with love or its facade

Really they are waiting to fall asleep
hoping they will not dream about hope
of any kind

These Are Your Doctors

by Johanna Shapiro

These are your doctors
drinking themselves into oblivion
jumping off rooftops
huddled sobbing on a bridge
sinking to the floor
outside their patients' rooms
They know how to choose
just the right drugs
to make the world disappear
They know exactly where
to place the gun

They look dazed, amazed
at their own
fragility
They do not want to be here
taking care of you
They think you are dying
and they are not
they pity you

Pity them, your doctors
They are filled with despair
that they don't recognize
because they cannot even recognize
your despair

See yourself in them
Then maybe they will see
themselves in you

Life from the Other Side of the Tray
by Pamela Shea

In a crowded emergency room
I am plastered against the back wall.
My husband, who usually stands tall
Now looks small on the table, pale and barely breathing.

I told them I'd been a medical assistant,
So they've let me stay in the back of the room,
Which is uncomfortably crowded
With personnel, all sensing urgency.

Thankfully, on my cell phone
I have a snapshot of our Covid vaccinations,
And I made a quick list of his medications
Before driving him to the nearest hospital.

Suddenly, a gleaming tray appears,
And I know the instruments it holds,
Sharp and bold for a clean incision.
The doctor's decision has been made
To open the obstructed airway.

My days of surgical assisting are done,
And though procedures intrigued me once, not now.
I start to edge my way out to leave the room,
For gloom and fear are seeping in.

I stop, directly facing the doctor.
We exchange a direct and intense look.
The narrative of the book changes
As he says, "Let's wait a minute."

The medicine kicks in and does its job.
Breath returns to all in that cramped room.
The looming specter of suffocation leaves
As sighs of relief sweep grief out the door.

Absent and Present
by Rodica Stan

I came home, father, but I have missed you.
COVID has kidnapped you, for good, and
I can only replay ad infinitum that last phone call and
That last FaceTime minute, you of breathless words, so lonely,
Waving from an ambulance bed on the way to your final home.

I came home, father, months after you'd left us.
Looking for your presence, fighting your absence,
Not able to cry in front of your tombstone, and
Not able to unmiss you in the garden, overcome by words,
By the book stack on your bedside, by your coffee cup on the table.

I felt your absence, where you were, in the cemetery,
I felt your presence where you were not, on the right side of the
sofa,
In the henhouse picking fresh eggs for our simple family dinners,
Under my arm walking to the market to buy peppers,
In the pictures of us from decades ago, exploring the Carpathian
Mountains.

I am at home, father, alone with your absence and your presence,
With the poems you scribbled like prayers in your notebook,
Mourning you and millions we have let go in the chokehold of
COVID.
Why have we, the world, broken into many
When we fought one virus?

Status Update
by Rodica Stan

I am healthy. Sanitized. Masked. Vaccinated. Alive.
My tears collect in empty espresso cups,
As I mourn my father's death, alone, asphyxiated,
As I fear my mother's death, alone, across
An ocean and two continents from me.

There is COVID everywhere,
In the space among us, them, all…
Infiltrating the air, our intellect,
History, death, and the earth that inters us.
S.O.S.

Dust
by Rodica Stan

...on white shirts stiffened in the closet
...on purple lipstick buried in the vanity box
...on the travel bag paralyzed under the bed
...on the picnic basket starving in the pantry

There was dust in my car's gas tank,
Dust on the car's roof and on the oak tree
That cast a shade net on it.
Stale dust cloaked my throat.

My father's body succumbed to the COVID virus.
His power vanished like a shadow before sunset.
His breath folded inwards
Like an erratic kite punished by the hurricane.

Virus, dust, virus, dust! A demonic waltz stepping on a
palimpsest... *MANUSCRIPT- ORIG WRITING EFFACED TO MK ROOM FOR*
LATER WRITING, BUT TRACES OF ORIG. REMAIN .
Of father's smile when I boarded the plane to move overseas...
Of the walk in the blooming linden forest of his childhood...
Of his hand wave on my phone screen on his last day...

Oblivion

by Bethlehem Tesfaye

You thought your glances would feed my soul
And I took them willingly, starved.
Like eating steaming food before it cools,
I found truth in the burn, reality marred.

DEMONS

You knew what little would keep me around,
And I came to it like a beacon,
Ignoring every sign, every sound
Of trouble, of fear, of reason.

It wasn't until the lost pandemic year.
The eerie silence that marked the unknown,
When I stared down demons I'd once feared
Quarantined with me in a room of my own.

So I wrote you slowly onto the page
To make sense to me what was hidden:
Your patterns, your actions, your intricate cage.
Until I wrote you into oblivion.

Giving Birth Just Before Lock Down
by Baotran N. Vo

Every day I read the news,
as I nurse my newborn
Every day I watch the covid count in our hospital
as I receive care for my own wounds
Every day I review our team briefing and call assignment
as I clean my mother's tracheotomy tube.

Every day I worry about my colleagues in the trenches, and their
high-risk families
as I teach my own high-risk father how to wear a mask.

Every day my wound is healing, and I prepare to return to the
trenches
The physician in me is ready to gown up and join the fight
The mother and daughter in me are terrified
I can be the solution to helping patients recover
But I can also be the vector, and the reason for my family's demise
I'm ready to return, but I'm not ready.

Every day I follow vaccine progress, as our covid census rises
As I see patients in tents
As I see families gather in black on the hospital lawn
I gown up, mask up, wash hands. Shower, and change before
getting home
I worry the milk that I pump for my baby may be contaminated
I worry that my hug could give my child the disease
I live in a mask, even as I sleep, nursing my baby
I try to do the right thing, doubting if I made the right call.

I take the vaccine at the first availability
I'd even take it in my eyeballs, if it's the only way
I look to the future with hope as our covid census dwindles
My heart full of joy, as our hospital tent is dismantled.

The Song I Still Long to Hear
by Melody Wang

You preferred early morning hikes, our plumed breaths echoing
       a slow-curling cascade mingling with pale winter sunlight

the cold air activating parts of us not accustomed to the realm
       beyond comfort, unease, or even the dull pain of the ages

melding into the sacred silence of remembrance and revealing
       the connection to what we had forgotten far beneath the
       surface.

The day your words ceased to form, the cold-preserved melody
       tinged with sorrow you swallowed thereafter. Still it eludes
       me

why I was chosen to witness love, loss, the great beyond —
       why you were chosen to be a silent embodiment of all three.

Originally published in a limited edition (50-copies), *Gnashing Teeth* winter
zine, 2021.

Face Time
By Peter Young

I held an iPad for Miguel as he lay in his hospital bed
so he could see his family sheltered at home.
He was suffocating, this man who at the worst of times
would only tell his loved ones, *Me siento bien.*
All around us the equipment of life
and death was buzzing, humming, beeping,
a stubborn choir of mockingbirds.

I turned the camera on myself so they could see
the plastic shield, the gown, the precious N95.
Outside, a train pulled away from Marble Hill; the city was fleeing.
Sunlight gleamed down the Harlem River, catching the red oaks
just starting to get their leaves back. It was blinding.
It was the first day that felt like spring.

I saw a dozen family members on my screen, squeezed
into a small apartment somewhere in Washington Heights.
A man my age held a young girl in the air; it seemed important
that I see her. She was laughing. Another man rose
to his feet and began to clap. Soon the whole room
was doing this. Someone whooped — for me! What gratitude,
like a prayer over my meager talent. I understood
they expected me to save him.

Miguel turned sixty-six in the ICU. His family gathered
outside his window to release balloons into the sky. I watched
as they sailed over northern Manhattan. Later that night
his daughter called and asked me to sing "happy birthday" to him.
And I did.

Tranquilo, I learned to say, *todo va estar bien.* I was lying
in a second language. There are few roads back
from where Miguel's body had gone, his lungs
full of something like cement. The rest fell
in sequence: kidneys, heart, then brain. From the start I knew
that when he died it would be like this, alone and pierced
with tubes. When his monitor stopped beeping, I peeled
his name tag from the door and let my intern
call his daughter. I walked home down Dyckman
still in my scrubs as neighbors leaned from windows
banging pots and pans, swinging *matracas*, making noise for me.
A virus is such a tiny thing
to demand so much from us.

Originally published in *The BEAT,* a medical-student magazine at UCLA.
Republished in *The SUN Magazine,* December 2021.
FaceTime | By Peter Young | Issue 552 | The Sun Magazine

Grateful for Time
by Shannon Zhang

I woke up at 5:30 a.m. Pen light, Pocket Medicine, and pens carefully placed in my white coat pockets as I walked toward the medical center, preparing myself mentally for the day. It was my first week of residency on the wards service and I was both excited and nervous. I was introduced to a patient that morning, Ms. W., who had been downgraded to our service from the medical intensive care unit.

She was diagnosed with stage IV pancreatic cancer several months ago and was admitted for abdominal pain and distention. Upon having a nasogastric tube placed through her nose for decompression, 3.5 liters of blood was expelled. The gastroenterology team performed an emergent scope and cauterized a large bleeding ulcer. When I approached her bed, I introduced myself as Doctor Zhang, still apprehensive about using the word "doctor." She turned her head up to look at me, remarked on how many doctors she had seen that day, and asked to be left alone.

As an incoming intern, I focused heavily on the "to do's": how many notes I'd have to write today, what orders I'd need to place, how many patients I'd need to discharge, and how to prepare for my presentations. With my list of things to do and her unwillingness to see me on my mind, I took a brief history and physical, made sure she was stable, and rushed out the door to see my remaining seven patients.

Week after week, I saw Ms. W. every morning. Some days, she had breakfast and cracked jokes. Other days, she asked to be left alone to sleep. Overall, though, she seemed to be improving and we had planned for her to be discharged to a skilled nursing facility to improve her functional capacity for a second round of chemotherapy.

A few days prior to her discharge, she began complaining of worsening abdominal pain and stopped eating, symptoms that I thought were associated with her pancreatic cancer. We ordered imaging and saw a large pneumoperitoneum in her abdomen.

She became more delirious over the next few days. The emergent surgery team told us she was not a surgical candidate and had 48-72 hours to live due to an abdominal perforation that could have occurred at any point during her hospitalization. We transitioned her to comfort care, giving her morphine and Zofran when she needed. Luckily, she made it past the 72-hour mark that was estimated by the surgery team. However, with each passing day, Ms. W. became less and less interested in engaging in conversation with me, and more and more interested in sleeping.

As days went by, I found myself wanting to stay longer with her during my pre-rounds. Most days, she slept as I held her hand and removed excess gauzes and bandages on her upper extremities as she complained about their discomfort. Despite my head running with the "to do's" of that day and her unwillingness to engage in conversation with me due to fatigue, I stayed with her as she slept peacefully. We invited her family to come visit, transitioned her to home hospice, and set her up for discharge.

During my last day on service, I greeted Ms. W. one last time, leaving her room before she could see my tears. I thought back to my first day with her and how I hastily swept out of her room to accomplish my tasks. Ms. W. reminded me about the humanism aspect of medicine: sitting by her side when she was lonely, removing excess bandages to make her more comfortable, and spending a few extra minutes with her even with the many other things to complete that day.

Thankful for the experience, I talked to her family one last time on the phone, feeling grateful that Ms. W. could be comfortable back home.

AUTHORS' GALLERY

Riya Bansal

Erica Duh

Anna Dunlap

Michael Eselun

Chloie Limpin Flores

Carol Grabowski

Jane Hilary

Lisa C. Krueger

Alexandra M. Levine

Frank L. Meyskens, Jr.   Gabriella Miotto   Stacy R. Nigliazzo

Kathleen Powers   Chalat Rajaram   Jose L. Recio

Jo Marie Reilly   Lorna Rodriguez-   Steven T. Rosen
                    Rodriguez

Johanna Shapiro   Pamela Shea   Rodica Stan

Bethlehem Tesfaye   Baotran N. Vo   Melody Wang

Peter Young   Shannon Zhang

ABOUT THE AUTHORS

Riya Bansal is a second- year medical student at the University of California, Irvine School of Medicine. She received a BS degree in Neurobiology, Physiology, and Behavior from University of California, Davis. There, she took a poetry class and discovered her passion for reading and writing poetry. Some of her interests in medicine include holistic medicine, serving underprivileged communities, and medical humanities.

Erica Duh, MD, is an internal medicine physician resident at UC Irvine. She grew up in the Washington, D.C./Maryland area, received her Bachelor of Science from Duke University, and spent three years teaching high school chemistry in California. After witnessing the health disparities in the community where she taught, she returned to medical school at Brown University. She is currently serving as Chief Resident in the 2021-2022 year, after which she hopes to pursue a gastroenterology fellowship.

Anna Dunlap is a part-time caregiver for a loved one with Alzheimer's, a member of the Laguna Poets, avid traveler, and community volunteer for causes dear to her heart. She received a Master's degree in Human Resources Economics from the University of Utah. During her career, she counseled developmentally disabled adults; served as public education policy advisor to a state governor; and led executive communications at several companies in the healthcare industry. Now retired, she unwittingly followed Rilke's advice to "wait and gather sense and sweetness for a whole lifetime" before attempting to write "ten good lines" of poetry. She is inching toward those ten good lines while making time for the important relationships in her life. Her poetry has been published in *The Colorado Sun* (2021) and *An Uncertain Age: Poems by Bold Women of a Certain Age* (Ink Sisters Press, 2021).

Michael Eselun, (he/him) **BCC** (Board Certified Chaplain), earned a BA degree in Design from UCLA, and decades later, completed an internship for chaplaincy at UCLA Medical Center. He was named the Dr. John Glaspy Chaplain in Oncology Care for the Simms/Mann-UCLA Center for Integrative Oncology-- a role he has filled for 12 years. In addition to oncology, he has worked extensively in palliative, hospice, and acute psychiatric care. Two-time TED-X speaker, he speaks extensively to healthcare professionals, patient populations, and faith communities across the country about the deeper questions of life, mortality, and meaning. He's been widely published in journals, including *Journal of Pastoral Care and Counseling*. He is an activist/educator addressing anti- LGBTQ bias in the larger community for over 30 years and was recently inducted into the UCLA-Semel Institute Eudaimonia Society. More information is available at www.michaeleselun.com .

Chloie Limpin Flores is a recent UCI graduate with a BS in Pharmaceutical Sciences. She is currently pursuing medicine and will be applying in the next cycle in Spring 2022. Her long-term goal is to specialize in oncology. In her free time, she shadows an oncologist, volunteers at an outreach clinic in Orange, and also at St. Joseph's Hospital, where she just finished the COPE Health Scholars program. She is also employed as a medical assistant for a gastroenterologist in Newport, CA and Fountain Valley, CA. In Summer 2021, she participated in the UCI Anti-Cancer Challenge, making campaign videos. She's been writing poetry since high school but only recently has she been public about her work. As a novice, she is excited to join the poetry community and learn new ways to express her message.

Carol J. Grabowski, MD, MBA received her degree from Temple University Medical School in Philadelphia, PA. She is a board-certified Obstetrician/Gynecologist who has been in practice at Long Beach Memorial since 1985. She trained at Temple University Medical School and The Medical College of Philadelphia. Until 2013, she was in private practice providing a full range of OB/GYN services including robotic minimally invasive surgery. As Director of Women's Health Services at The Children's Clinic, she expanded their OB/GYN for underinsured and uninsured women in Long Beach. Caring for this multicultural population has required communicating in as many as four languages in one day. She is a long-term Board Member of the Women's Shelter of Long Beach; and regularly engages in group education and public forums.

Jane Hilary is a graduate of Healing Hands School of Holistic Health (HHP, 2005). Over the last few years, she has retired from an eclectic career as an acting teacher, actor, arts administrator and holistic health practitioner. She has written poetry since the age of sixteen in a genre identified and coined in 2010 by poet Ricki Mandeville as *creative, therapeutic retrospective*. Her poetry has been published in the *California Quarterly* (California State Poetry Society, 2021); and in *Pop Art: An Anthology of Southern California Poets* (Moon Tide Press, 2010). Jane currently credits her family, the natural world, and friends—including the Laguna Poets--as her source of inspiration, as she explores collective healing through the honoring of personal freedoms and the heroic journey of the individual.

Lisa C. Krueger, PhD, MFA, is a clinical psychologist and poet in Pasadena. Her poems have appeared in various journals, including *Ploughshares, Alaska Quarterly Review, Rattle,* and *Prairie Schooner*. She has published articles on imagery and parallels between poetry and therapy. Her fourth collection of poems with Red Hen Press, *Run Away to the Yard,* was published in 2017. She maintains a therapy practice with a focus on girls' and women's issues, health psychology, and writing therapy.

Alexandra M. Levine, MD, MACP, is a Professor at the City of Hope National Medical Center, and was Chief Medical Officer from 2007-2017. Prior, she was Chief, Division of Hematology at Keck School of Medicine, USC, where she was a Distinguished Professor of Medicine; the Bloom Family Chair in Lymphoma; and the Medical Director of the USC/Norris Cancer Hospital. She served as Executive Associate Dean of the USC School of Medicine from 1985 through 1990. Dr. Levine is a nationally and internationally recognized authority on the malignancies associated with HIV, as well as on HIV in women. She worked with Jonas Salk on the development and testing of a therapeutic AIDS vaccine. She was appointed to the Presidential HIV/AIDS Advisory Council by President Clinton in 1995, serving as Chair of the Research Committee. She has served as Consultant to the Health Departments of Chile, Russia, India, and China in terms of HIV/AIDS. Dr. Levine has published 325 scientific articles, 65 chapters, and has edited two books. She served on the Board of Scientific Counselors of the NCI, and on the Oncologic Drug Advisory Committee of the FDA. She was elected a Master of the American College of Physicians in 2009. She received her MD degree from University of Southern California.

Dr. Frank L. Meyskens, Jr., MD, FACP, is Distinguished Professor of Medicine Emeritus and Founding Director of the NCI-nationally designated Comprehensive Cancer Center at the University of California, Irvine; and is a Physician Scientist internationally renowned for translationally based laboratory studies. More of his bio can be seen in **ABOUT THE EDITORS** section that follows.

Gabriella Miotto, **MD,** trained in medicine at McGill University in Montreal, Quebec; family medicine at UC Irvine; and public health at UCLA. Her work as a family physician has focused on community medicine in California and Alaska, as well as humanitarian relief and development work internationally in Latin America and the Balkans, with such groups as PROSECO, the UNHCR, and Doctors of the World. She is a family physician at the community clinic "TCC Family Health" in Long Beach, CA, and is an active member of the Laguna Poets Workshop, in Laguna Beach, CA. Her poetry has been published in the following anthologies: *Plague 2020: COVID-19 Art and Poetry from Around the World,* edited by Mahnaz Badihian (MahMag, 2020); *Nasty Women and Bad Hombres: A Poetry Anthology* (Lascaux Editions 2017); *Pop Art: An Anthology of Southern California Poetry* (Moon Tide Press, 2010). Her current interests lie in the realms of nature, the imagination, medicine, poetry, dream-tending, earth practices, and how body and psyche partner with each other for wellness and healing through imagery.

Stacy R. Nigliazzo, RN, an emergency room nurse in Texas, is the award-winning author of *Scissored Moon* and *Sky the Oar* (Press 53). Her poems have appeared in the *Bellevue Literary Review, Beloit Poetry Journal, Ploughshares*, and *JAMA*, among other publications. She is co-poetry editor of *Pulse, Voices from The Heart of Medicine*. She was hand-selected to be the Keynote Speaker at the 5th Annual Symposium of Healing and Hope sponsored by UC Irvine in February 2022.

Kathleen Powers, PhD, is a medical student at UC Irvine School of Medicine. She graduated from the doctoral program in Rhetoric at UC Berkeley in 2020. "The Cybernetic Origins of Life" was the title of her dissertation. Her research has been supported by the Townsend Center for the Humanities at UC Berkeley and the UC Humanities Research Institute. She studies the organism in philosophy of biology.

Chalat Rajaram, MD, FAC, FAAHPM, CMD, HMDC, has been practicing Internal Medicine in Orange County for the past 30 years. Dr. Rajaram joined Vitas Healthcare in 2006 and became its Medical Director in 2008. Until his retirement from VITAS Healthcare in June, 2021, Dr. Rajaram was the External Faculty Director for the University of California, Irvine (UCI) palliative care fellowship program. He is certified by the Hospice Medical Directors Certification Board; is a Fellow of the American Academy of Hospice and Palliative Medicine; is Board-Certified in Internal Medicine; and is a Fellow of the American College of Physicians. His interest in Geriatric medicine grew in his office practice and later in the care of elder patients in Nursing and Rehabilitation facilities. A Certified Medical Director (American Board of Post-Acute and Long-Term Care Medicine), he has been serving as Medical Director at Newport Nursing & Rehabilitation Center in Newport Beach, CA, since 2004. He was awarded the 2018 Meals on Wheels Orange County Physician of the Year honor at the organization's annual gala. He currently serves on the Board of Directors, Meals on Wheels OC.

Jose L Recio, MD, was born and raised in Spain, where he studied medicine and worked in neurosciences. He left Spain for California on an International Fellowship. In California, Dr. Recio specialized in psychiatry. While in practice, he published several papers in specialized journals. Over the last few years, however, he has developed an interest in creative writing. He has recently published a book of fiction: *Transitions: Twenty-Four Bilingual Short Stories* (Adelaide Books: New York & Lisbon). He writes both in Spanish and English. He and his wife currently live in Los Angeles.

Jo Marie Reilly, MD, MPH, is a Professor of Family Medicine at the Keck School of Medicine of USC (KSOM). She completed her Master's degree in public health at USC's Keck School of Medicine in 2017. She graduated from Georgetown Medical School and completed her internship and residency in family medicine at the Kaiser Permanente Family Residency Program in Los Angeles. She completed a fellowship in women's health and obstetrics at the White Memorial Family Practice Residency Program. Dr. Reilly is the Vice-Chair of Education in the KSOM Department of Family; the Director of the KSOM's Primary Care Initiative; and the KSOM Family Medicine Pre-Doctoral Director. She is past chair of the American Academy of Family Physician's Commission on Education, Student and Resident subcommittee and also serves on the medical humanities editorial boards of Family Systems and Health and PULSE, lessons from the heart. Dr. Reilly's publications and research interests include developing a primary care workforce, inter-professional care teams, physician well-being, care of the underserved, medical arts and humanities, and women and children's health. Learn more at www.jmreilly@med.usc.edu .

Lorna Rodríguez-Rodríguez, MD, is a native of Puerto Rico where she grew up and earned her medical degree. She came to the mainland pursuing postgraduate education, and received a Ph.D. in biochemistry at the University of Rochester, where she won a medal with the Bloom Award for the best dissertation in Biochemistry. She completed her specialty in Obstetrics and Gynecology at Rutgers University, and a Gynecologic Oncology subspecialty at University

110

of Michigan. She has held several leadership roles in her field, such as Chief of Gynecologic Oncology at University of Rochester and Rutgers University; Director of Precision Medicine at Rutgers; and, most recently, Vice-Chair of Surgery at a major cancer center in California. She is recognized for her scientific work in ovarian cancer as well as her clinical expertise. She also actively works in the Diversity, Inclusion and Equity Council at the City of Hope and is particularly passionate about bringing more leaders of color to the institution. She writes about health inequities and the role of medical professionals in the well-being of their communities and their own mental and physical health.

Steven T. Rosen, MD, FACP, FASCO, is the Provost, Chief Scientific Officer, and Director of the Comprehensive Cancer Center and the Beckman Research Institute, Irell & Manella Cancer Center Director's Distinguished Chair for the City of Hope in Duarte, CA. Following his graduation with distinction from Northwestern University Medical School's Six-Year Honors Program in Chicago, IL, Dr. Rosen completed his residency in internal medicine at Northwestern. Among the many leadership posts he has held are Director of the Robert H. Lurie Comprehensive Cancer Center at Northwestern University; Chair and board member of the Medical Science Committee of the LLS; Editor-in-Chief of *Cancer Treatment and Research*; and Board Member of American Society of Clinical Oncology's Conquer Cancer Foundation. His career has been graced with many awards, including Northwestern University Medical School's Alumni Achievement Award (1994); the Martin Luther King Humanitarian Award from Northwestern Memorial Hospital (1995); Israel Cancer Research Fund, Man of Distinction Award (2011); and Lifetime Achievement Award (2015). He has also been named to the list "Best Doctors in Chicago" as well as in Los Angeles. Dr. Rosen's laboratory research focuses on experimental therapeutics and hematologic malignancies. He has published more than 400 scientific papers and has been an advisor to more than two dozen NCI Comprehensive Cancer Centers. His poetry has appeared in the anthologies *Stolen Moments* (2007) and *Heartfelt Reflections* (2021).

Johanna Shapiro, MA, PhD, is Professor Emerita of Family Medicine and Founder-Director of the Program in Medical Humanities & Arts, University of California, Irvine, School of Medicine. She is the recipient of many teaching awards and honors. More of her bio can be seen in **ABOUT THE EDITORS** section that follows.

Pamela Shea was the 9th Poet-Laureate of Sunland-Tujunga, CA, where she enjoyed "taking poetry to the people" at many venues around the community. She participated in the "Gathering of California's Poets Laureate" at McGroarty Arts Center, hosted by California State Poet Laureate Dana Gioia in 2018. Her poetry has been published in journals and anthologies across California, including *We Are Here Village Poets Anthology, Altadena Poetry Review Anthology,* and *The Cherita.* Her professional life has included medical office work and teaching in the fitness field. Pam studied at the University of Redlands.

Rodica Stan, PhD, was born in a small remote town in Romania. She left home at age 18 to study Biochemistry at the University of Bucharest, and received a PhD in Biochemistry and Molecular Biology in 1998 from Rutgers University, in New Jersey. Stepping right into research in academia in a foreign country came with the challenges of a new work environment, a new language, and a new culture. Writing essays, poems, and a memoir balanced Rodica's life and has continued to give her personal satisfaction. Rodica is a blogger and has published two personal essays in *Science* magazine. This is the first time her poems appear in print.

Bethlehem Tesfaye is currently a second-year medical student at the University of California, Irvine School of Medicine. Her degree is expected in 2024. Her passion for medicine is only rivaled by that of language, with reading and writing poetry serving as a refuge of self-reflection for her. One of her poems, "Forbidden," was published in *Life (as it) Happens: A Nerdfighter Poetry Book* (Nikki Williamson

Publishing, 2018), an anthology created to raise funds for multiple international non-profit organizations.

Baotran N. Vo, MD, is a Family Medicine physician and an Associate Clinical Professor at the University of California, Irvine. She practices and teaches broad spectrum Family Medicine, including outpatient and inpatient care of all genders and age groups, in-office procedures, family planning, prenatal care, labor and delivery, and newborn care. She is also the Medical Director for UCI's student-run free clinic that teaches students and residents community-centered care and volunteerism. Her two children were her inspirations for various creative works, including her poems "Late" and "Post-Call Parent" that were featured in University of California, Irvine's annual medical arts and humanities publication, *Plexus*.

Melody Wang, MSW, obtained her Master's degree in Social Work at the University of Southern California. She is currently a Research Operations Analyst at City of Hope. Writing poetry is an important part of her life, with her debut chapbook, *Night-Blooming Cereus,* published by Alien Buddha Press in December 2021. Her poetry has been published, or is forthcoming, in various journals and anthologies, including *Neologism Poetry Journal, Trouvaille Review, West Trestle Review, Eclectica Magazine, The Wild Word, One Art Poetry Journal, and Hobart After Dark.* Her poem, "The Song I Still Long to Hear," was published in the *Gnashing Teeth* limited edition hard-copy winter zine in 2021.

Peter Young, MD, is a primary care and HIV physician working at UCLA in the Extensivist Program. He completed his internal medicine training at Columbia University in New York and worked as a senior resident during the COVID-19 pandemic in New York City. He has studied narrative medicine and teaches an introductory workshop in narrative medicine for Internal Medicine residents at UCLA. In his free time, he enjoys rock climbing and exploring the outdoors around Los Angeles.

Shannon Zhang, MD, is a second-year internal medicine resident at the University of California, Irvine Medical Center and plans to pursue a career in the field of hematology and oncology. She attended undergraduate school in San Diego, CA, prior to moving to Tucson, AZ for medical training at the University of Arizona School of Medicine. Her interest in oncology first stemmed from performing oncology research during her undergraduate years. Now, she is most attracted to the special patient and physician relationship that the field offers. She hopes that her essay in this anthology can help remind healthcare providers of the humanism aspect of medicine, especially during these trying times of the pandemic.

ABOUT THE EDITORS

Thelma T. Reyna, PhD, received an MA in English/Minor in Psychology from Texas A&I University in Kingsville, TX; an MA in Educational Administration from California State University, L.A.; and a doctoral degree in Educational Leadership from UCLA. Her poetry, short fiction, and nonfiction have collectively won 20 national and international book awards. She has written 6 books—a short story collection, 2 poetry chapbooks, 2 full-length poetry collections, and a memoir in poetry—and edited 3 award-winning anthologies. She was Poet Laureate in Altadena, CA, in 2014-2016 and edited the *Altadena Poetry Review Anthology* in both those years. In 2020, she also edited *When the Virus Came Calling: COVID-19 Strikes America,* a national award-winning anthology of 46 distinguished authors and prose writers from across the U.S. that depicted the first 7 months of the pandemic in real time in poetry, personal essays, and a short story. It received 5 book honors in 2020-2021, with the most recent being a Silver Medal in the Nonfiction/Political Issues category of the International Latino Book Awards. Dr. Reyna was a Pushcart Prize Nominee in Poetry in 2017.

Dr. Frank L. Meyskens, Jr., MD, FACP, is Distinguished Professor of Medicine Emeritus and Founding Director of the NCI-nationally designated Comprehensive Cancer Center at the University of California, Irvine; a Physician Scientist internationally renowned for translationally based laboratory studies of redox chemistry and cancer; co-founder of the field of chemo-prevention for AACR, ASCO, and SWOG; and co-developer of several clinical chemoprevention companies. Since 2001, he has helped develop the field of end-of-life medicine. Dr. Meyskens has attained international prominence for his poetic contributions and his co-editorship of a column in *Oncology Times* titled "Poetry for Cancer Caregivers." He has published in different academic venues, including in his blog ASCO Connection "White Coat Conversations," and was designated as Poet Laurate for ASCO. He has published two books of patient, care-giver , and family -themed poetry (*Aching for Tomorrow* and *Believing in Today*). In 2018 he co-organized the well-received "1st Annual Symposium on Healing and Hope," which continues with the 5th Annual Symposium in February 2022.

Johanna Shapiro, MA, PhD, is Professor Emerita of Family Medicine and Founder-Director of the Program in Medical Humanities & Arts, University of California, Irvine, School of Medicine. She is the recipient of many teaching awards and honors, including STFM's Humanism in Medicine Award in 2020 and UCI's Lauds & Laurels Outstanding Faculty Achievement award. Dr. Shapiro's research and scholarship focus on the process of professional identity formation in medical education, including the impact of training on student empathy, on medical student-patient relationships, and on the management of difficult clinical encounters. She is widely published in the field of medical humanities. Her book, *The Inner World of Medical Students: Listening to Their Voices in Poetry,* is a critical analysis of important themes in the socialization process of medical students as expressed through their creative writing. She has published poetry in several journals, including *Pulse, The Healing Muse, Journal of General Internal Medicine,* and *JAMA.* She is co-founder and co-coordinator of the "Annual Symposium on Healing and Hope" series hosted by the University of California, Irvine.

ACKNOWLEDGMENTS

By Thelma T. Reyna, PhD

Collaborating with Frank Meyskens and Johanna Shapiro in editing and producing this anthology has been a wondrous journey filled with mutual enlightenment and fulfillment. They had asked me to be Keynote Speaker at their annual symposium of Hope & Healing in 2021, then followed that up with an invitation to join them as a co-coordinator of the event planned for 2022. Thus began our teamwork that led ultimately to this book.

We saw a connection between the work and goals of the symposium and the act of bringing together the lived experiences of pandemic fighters who find time in their healing professions to create poetry and thoughtful personal essays that help them process and navigate the challenges and losses they bear. I thank Frank and Johanna for their vision in making this book a reality.

My gratitude, also, to the 26 medical professionals who shared their writings with us...and now, with the world. They have opened windows into their work, their mission, and their deeply caring hearts. Bravo to these heroes!

By Frank L. Meyskens, Jr., MD

The long career path leading to my co-editorship of this anthology has been deeply influenced by my clinical practice, laboratory research, and history of complex personal illnesses over the 30 years that I have been on the faculty at University of California, Irvine. Hundreds of colleagues, staff, and patients have affected this odyssey. A few of those providing important stability to this rocky journey include administrators Tom Cesario, Sidney Golub, Michael Gottfredson, and Elizabeth Yi. Critical long term staff support included Janis DeJohn, Feng Liu- Smith, and Angela Garcia. I specifically thank volunteer Jacquie Tidball for her superb administrative assistance over the past year during the creation of this anthology.

My family has long provided a safe haven even during the most tumultuous of times. My three children: daughter Moriah, her husband Dany, and their sons Dante, Enzo, and Tiago; son Covell, his wife Cindy, and their precious daughter Ya-Yen; and daughter Desy, her husband Facundo, and their sons Lucio, Diego, Bruno, and Mario. My brother Tom and sister Mary have also provided meaningful continuity throughout the years.

Finally, Linda, my wife, muse, and healing anodyne, has been there every day of every year, allowing me to shine and to survive when the light had almost gone out. Forever may we walk hand-in-hand into the future and whatever it may hold.

By Johanna Shapiro, PhD

The collaborative process is something often praised but less often successful in practice. I feel extremely fortunate to have had the opportunity to collaborate in the true spirit of the word with my long-term colleague, Dr. Frank Meyskens, and my newer but equally valued colleague, Dr. Thelma Reyna. From Frank, I learned the importance of grand vision; and from Thelma, the importance of attention to every single word. I am forever grateful for their professional companionship on this journey.

I am also grateful for the unswerving support of the UC Irvine Department of Family Medicine over the past 22 years as I worked to build a program in medical humanities in the School of Medicine. In particular, my chair, Dr. Cindy Haq, and my colleague, Dr. Tan Nguyen, have been cherished partners in this endeavor. I am also deeply thankful to the many medical students who have taken the risk with me to reflect through arts and humanities on what medicine is and what it should be; as well as who they want to be as physicians and as people.

I am also very lucky to have three wonderful children who

put up with remarkable good grace with the twists and turns of my teaching, research and writing. Finally, I owe a great, unpayable debt to my husband of 52 years, who is my greatest booster, always showing me a path forward, and proving time and again that he knows me better than I know myself.

 **National Award-Winning Indie Literary Book Press**

Our indie-published books have earned over 22 national book honors. Visit our website to see our poetry collections, fiction, and non-fiction books at www.GoldenFoothillsPress.com

Our authors are available for literary events; book signings; classroom presentations in high school and college; book clubs; civic organizations; panel presentations; and as guest speaker or workshop presenter on varied topics.

Over 150 distinguished authors from across the United States have been published by our press since its founding in 2014, including Poets Laureate, Pushcart Prize Nominees, national and international book award winners, and recipients of many other regional and state honors. Visit our website to see listings of our authors.

Contact Chief Editor/Publisher
Thelma T. Reyna, Ph.D.
at www.GoldenFoothillsPress.com
goldenfoothillspress@ yahoo. com
Phone 626-375-5442

Space for Notes

Space for Notes

Space for Notes

Space for Notes

Space for Notes